SHARK

LIFE CYCLES

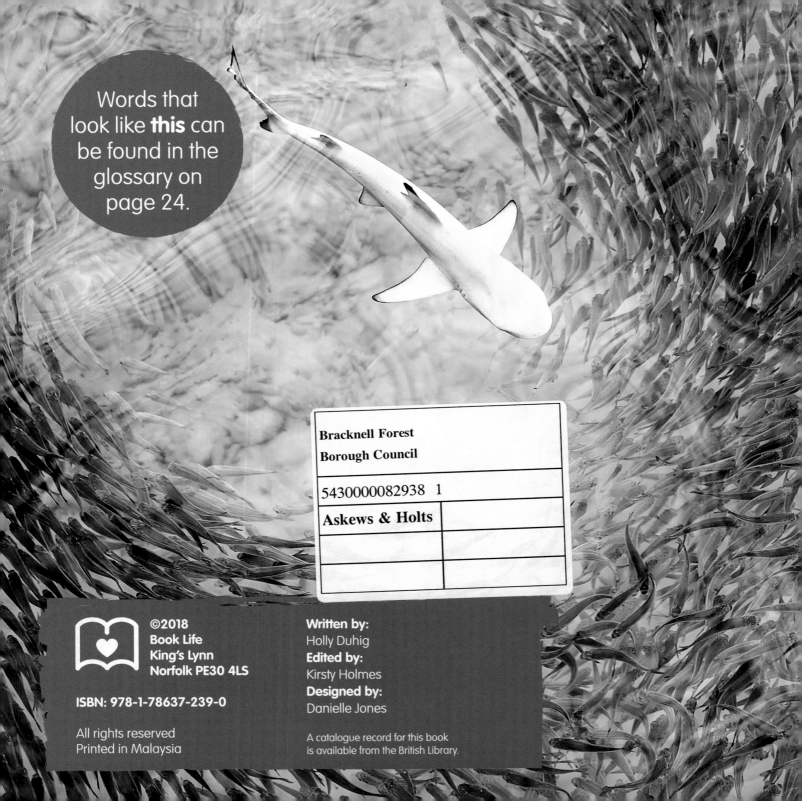

Words that look like **this** can be found in the glossary on page 24.

©2018
Book Life
King's Lynn
Norfolk PE30 4LS

ISBN: 978-1-78637-239-0

Written by:
Holly Duhig
Edited by:
Kirsty Holmes
Designed by:
Danielle Jones

A catalogue record for this book
is available from the British Library.

SHARK

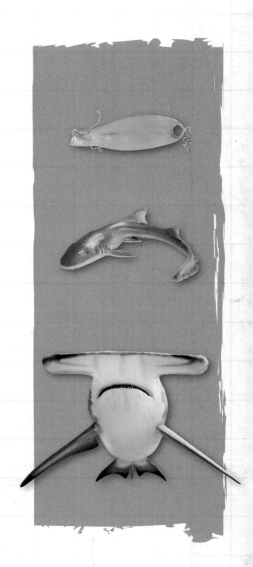

WHAT IS A LIFE CYCLE?

All animals, plants and humans go through different stages of their life as they grow and change. This is called a life cycle.

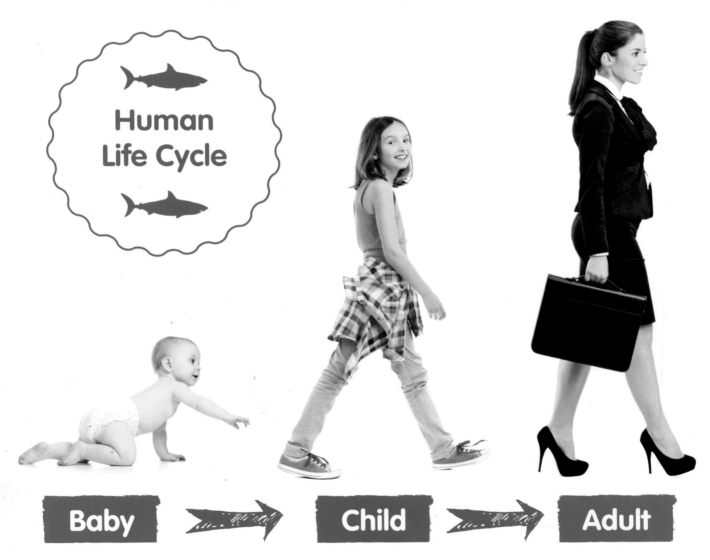

Human Life Cycle

Baby ➤ Child ➤ Adult

WHAT IS A SHARK?

A shark is a type of fish. It has **gills**, fins and sharp teeth.
Sharks hunt other fish. They are great **predators**.

EGGS

Most female sharks lay eggs, but some give birth to their **young**. Some **species** of shark only lay a few eggs but others can lay up to 100 eggs.

Female Shark

A female shark gives birth in a nursery. Nurseries are areas of warm, shallow water which are perfect for laying eggs and giving birth.

Some sharks lay their eggs in an egg case. These cases are tough and leathery, which help protect the shark's eggs.

Mermaid's Purse

Egg cases are sometimes called mermaid's purses.

Shark Eggs

While still in the egg, baby sharks feed on their egg's **yolk** for **nutrients**. Once they have eaten this, they might eat the other eggs around them.

PUPS

Shark Pup

Female sharks leave their eggs as soon as they have laid them. Baby sharks are called pups. Pups are not usually looked after by their mothers.

Pups have to hunt for food straight away. Because of this, they are born with a full set of teeth. Shark pups often stay together for protection from predators.

GROWING PUPS

Shark Pup in Coral Reef

Growing pups need lots of food. This is why shark nurseries are often in coral reefs, where there are lots of small fish for the pups to feed on.

Most sharks live for a long time. Because of this, pups are not in a hurry to grow up. Pups stay in their nurseries for a long time before swimming to deeper waters.

Bamboo
Shark Pups

SHARKS

Sharks jump out of the water when hunting for **prey**.

Adult sharks are fearsome predators. They can swim very fast and hunt large animals, such as seals and dolphins.

Sharks have large fins and powerful tails which make them extremely fast swimmers. Great white sharks can reach speeds of up to 48 kilometres per hour when hunting.

Great White Shark

SCARY SHARKS

Hammerhead
Sharks

One of the strangest looking sharks is the hammerhead
shark. They are called hammerhead sharks because of
their hammer-shaped heads, which have eyes at each end!

Basking sharks are the second largest fish in the world. These sharks' huge mouths look very scary, but don't worry – they only like eating **plankton**.

Plankton

Basking Shark

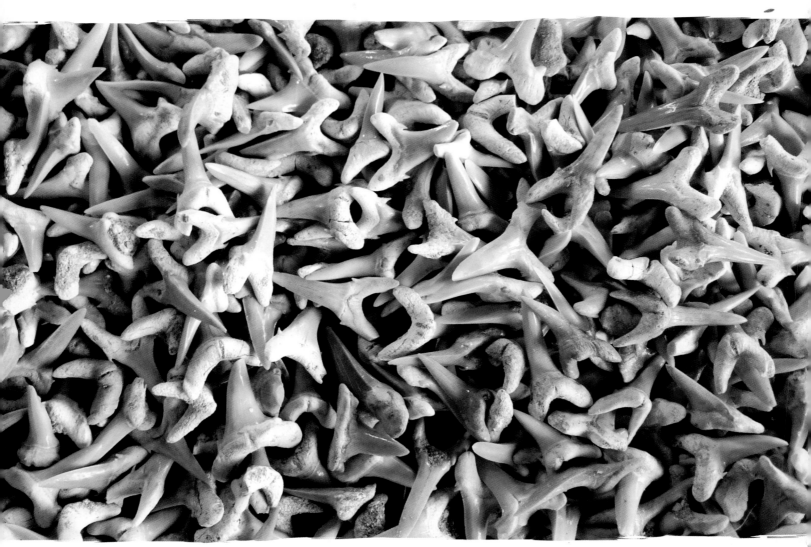

When sharks lose a tooth, a new one always grows in its place.
A shark can grow and lose up to 20,000 teeth in its lifetime.

Fear of sharks is called galeophobia.

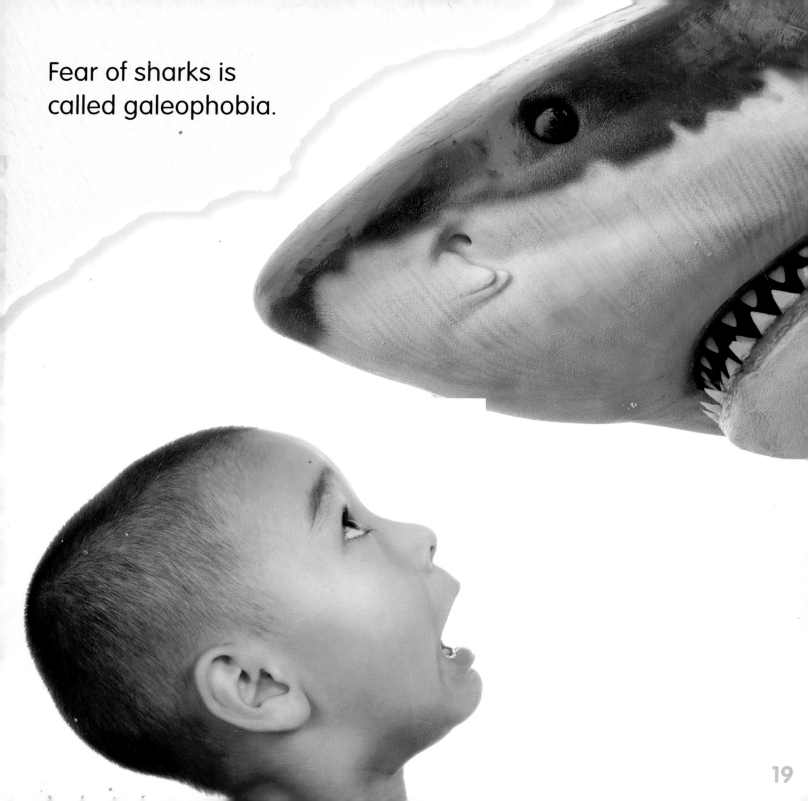

WORLD RECORD BREAKERS

Largest Shark

The largest species of shark ever to have lived was the Carcharodon megalodon. It was around 18 metres long with a two-metre-wide mouth. This species of shark is now **extinct**.

Shortfin Mako Shark

Fastest Swimmer

The fastest shark in the ocean is the shortfin mako shark. This shark can reach speeds of 67 kilometres per hour! It uses this speed to catch its favourite food — tuna fish.

LIFE CYCLE OF A SHARK

1

A female shark lays eggs or gives birth to her young.

2

The baby sharks eat their egg yolks, then hatch.

LIFE CYCLES

4

Adult sharks look for a **mate** so they can produce their own young.

3

The pups stay in the nursery until they are old enough to swim in deeper waters.

You can find out more about sharks by visiting an **aquarium**. Some aquariums have shark tanks where you can see and learn all about sharks.

GLOSSARY

aquarium   a place containing tanks of many different sea creatures

extinct   when a species of animal is no longer alive

gills   the organs that some animals use to breathe underwater

mate   a partner who an animal chooses to produce young with

nutrients   natural substances that plants and animals need to grow and stay healthy

plankton   microscopic creatures that float in the sea

predators   animals that hunt other animals for food

prey   animals that are hunted by other animals for food

species   a group of very similar animals or plants that are capable of producing young together

yolk   the nutritious part of an egg

young   an animal's offspring

INDEX

PHOTO CREDITS

Photocredits: Abbreviations: l-left, r-right, b-bottom, t-top, c-centre, m-middle.
Front Cover — Kletr. 1 — Kletr. 2 — mycamerawork. 3t – orhan senol, 3m – Evlakhov Valeriy, 3b – Kletr. 4l – Oksana Kuzmina. 4m – studioloco. 4r – Ljupco Smokovski. 5 – solarseven. 6 – Alessandro De Maddalena. 7 – frantisekhojdysz. 8 – jopelka. 9 – JoLin. 10 – johannviloria. 11 – UsulArt. 12 – Rich Carey. 13 – feathercollector. 14 – Alexyz3d. 15 – Andrea Izzotti. 16 – Alex Rush. 17 main – Grant M Henderson, 17 inset – Napat. 18 – Linnas. 19tr – Tanapipat Wongpinkaew, 19bl – 3445128471. 20 – Panda Vector. 21 – wildestanimal. 22t – Sergio Gosalvez, 22l – Flavio Palermo , 22b – Shane Gross, 22r – Fiona Ayerst. 23 – wavebreakmedia. Images are courtesy of Shutterstock.com. With thanks to Getty Images, Thinkstock Photo and iStockphoto.